Navigating Wealth

A Comprehensive Guide to Strategic Investments in Transportation

NAVIGATING WEALTH

First edition. November 27, 2023.

ISBN: 979-8223692133

Written by Ryan Sam.

Table of Contents

Ryan Sam

Chapter I: Introduction

A. Definition and Importance of Transport Investment

Transport investment, at its core, refers to the strategic allocation of resources to enhance and develop various modes of transportation, creating a network that facilitates the movement of people, goods, and services. This allocation includes funding for the construction, maintenance, and improvement of transportation infrastructure such as roads, railways, airports, seaports, and other critical components of a nation's transport system.

The importance of transport investment cannot be overstated, as it plays a fundamental role in shaping the economic, social, and environmental landscapes of a region or country. Here are key aspects that highlight the significance of transport investment:

Economic Catalyst:

Trade Facilitation: Efficient transportation systems reduce the cost and time associated with moving goods, promoting trade and economic growth. Well-developed infrastructure enhances a nation's competitiveness in the global market.

Job Creation: Transport investments, whether in the construction of new infrastructure or the maintenance of existing ones, generate employment opportunities across various skill levels, contributing to economic stability.

Connectivity and Accessibility:

Regional Integration: Transport links regions, fostering connectivity and integration. Well-connected transportation networks break down geographical barriers, promoting collaboration and resource sharing between different areas.

Accessibility: Improved transport infrastructure enhances accessibility, connecting remote areas to urban centers and providing communities with access to education, healthcare, and economic opportunities.

Efficiency and Productivity:

Supply Chain Optimization: An efficient transportation system streamlines the movement of goods, reducing supply chain costs and enhancing overall productivity for businesses.

Time Savings: Well-designed and maintained transport infrastructure reduces travel times, benefiting both individuals and businesses and increasing overall efficiency.

Social Impact:

Quality of Life: Transport investments contribute to improved quality of life by reducing traffic congestion, enhancing safety, and providing reliable modes of transportation for individuals.

Social Inclusion: Accessible transportation infrastructure ensures that all segments of the population, including those with mobility challenges, can participate in social and economic activities.

Environmental Considerations:

Sustainability: Modern transport investments increasingly focus on sustainable practices, such as the development of public transit systems, cycling lanes, and electric vehicle infrastructure, contributing to environmental conservation and mitigating the impact of transportation on climate change.

In essence, transport investment is a cornerstone of economic development, fostering connectivity, promoting efficiency, and shaping the overall well-being of societies. Recognizing its multifaceted impact, strategic and informed decisions in transport investment are essential for building resilient, sustainable, and prosperous communities.

B. The Evolution of Transportation and its Economic Impact

The evolution of transportation stands as a testament to humanity's ingenuity, adaptability, and pursuit of progress. From primitive modes of travel to the high-tech systems of today, each era has seen transportation evolve in response to societal needs, technological advancements, and economic demands.

Ancient and Early Modes of Transportation:

In ancient times, human mobility relied on simple yet ingenious forms of transportation, including walking, domesticated animals, and early forms of watercraft.

The Silk Road, established over 2,000 years ago, became a pivotal trade route, connecting the East and West and facilitating the exchange of goods, culture, and ideas.

The Era of Exploration and Maritime Expansion:

The Age of Exploration in the 15th to 17th centuries witnessed the advent of maritime navigation and the exploration of new lands. Ships played a crucial role in global trade, shaping the world economy and fostering cultural exchange.

The Industrial Revolution and Railways:

The 19th century marked a transformative period with the advent of steam-powered engines, particularly in the form of locomotives. Railways revolutionized transportation, connecting cities, enabling faster travel, and facilitating the mass movement of goods and people.

The Automobile and Personal Mobility:

The early 20th century brought about the mass production of automobiles, transforming personal mobility. Cars became accessible to the general public, reshaping urban planning and paving the way for suburbanization.

Aviation and Global Connectivity:

The development of aviation in the early 20th century enabled rapid long-distance travel. Airplanes not only revolutionized passenger transport but also became essential for global trade, connecting distant regions and facilitating international commerce.

Technological Advancements in the Late 20th Century:

The latter half of the 20th century witnessed technological breakthroughs, including the development of containerization in maritime transport, improving the efficiency of cargo handling and lowering shipping costs.

Digital Era and Smart Transportation:

The 21st century has seen the integration of digital technologies into transportation systems. Smart transportation includes innovations such as GPS navigation, ride-sharing apps, and real-time traffic management, enhancing efficiency and user experience.

Economic Impact of Transportation Evolution:

The evolution of transportation has had profound economic implications, shaping industries, trade patterns, and global economic structures.

Globalization: Improved transportation has facilitated the globalization of trade and commerce, allowing businesses to access global markets and consumers to enjoy a diverse range of products.

Supply Chain Optimization: Efficient transportation systems have optimized supply chains, reducing lead times and inventory costs for businesses across various industries.

Job Creation: Each phase of transportation evolution has generated employment opportunities, from the construction of railways and highways to the operation of airports and logistics services.

Urbanization and Economic Centers: Transportation developments have driven urbanization, concentrating economic activities in major metropolitan areas with well-connected transport infrastructure.

Innovation and Industry Growth: The transportation sector itself has become a source of innovation and economic growth, with industries related to aerospace, automotive, logistics, and technology contributing significantly to national economies.

In conclusion, the evolution of transportation is a dynamic force that has shaped societies and economies throughout history. Understanding this evolution is crucial for anticipating future trends, making informed investment decisions, and harnessing the economic potential of an ever-changing transportation landscape.

C. Purpose and Scope of the Book

The purpose and scope of "Navigating Wealth: A Comprehensive Guide to Strategic Investments in Transportation" are rooted in the recognition of the pivotal role that transport investments play in shaping economies, fostering connectivity, and driving sustainable development. This book aspires to serve as a guiding beacon for investors, policymakers, and enthusiasts navigating the intricate landscape of transportation investments.

Purpose:

Illuminate the Multifaceted Nature of Transport Investments:

This book aims to demystify the complexities of transport investments by providing a comprehensive exploration of various aspects, from traditional road infrastructure to cutting-edge technologies like autonomous vehicles and hyperloop systems.

Provide a Comprehensive Guide for Strategic Decision-Making:

Acting as a practical guide, the book endeavors to equip readers with the knowledge and tools necessary to make informed and strategic decisions in the realm of transportation investments. It seeks to empower readers to navigate challenges, assess risks, and identify opportunities for impactful investments.

Scope:

Comprehensive Coverage of the Transportation Landscape:

The scope of the book spans the entire spectrum of the transportation sector, encompassing traditional investments in road infrastructure, railways, airports, and maritime ports. It also extends to explore emerging opportunities in sustainable transport, electric and autonomous vehicles, high-speed rail, and drone delivery systems.

In-Depth Analysis of Risk Factors and Mitigation Strategies:

The book delves into risk analysis from multiple perspectives, addressing economic, technological, environmental, and regulatory risks associated with transport investments. Mitigation strategies are explored to assist readers in navigating uncertainties and ensuring the resilience of their investments.

Real-World Insights through Case Studies:

To offer practical insights, the book incorporates case studies highlighting both successful and unsuccessful transport investments. These case studies provide valuable lessons from the field, illustrating the factors that contribute to success and the pitfalls that investors should avoid.

Financial Modeling and Analysis:

A dedicated section of the book is devoted to financial modeling and analysis, covering essential topics such as cost-benefit analysis, return on investment (ROI) calculation, and various financing options, including public-private partnerships.

Exploration of Future Trends and Opportunities:

Anticipating the dynamic nature of the transportation industry, the book explores future trends and opportunities. This includes advancements in technology, the influence of policy and regulation, and the evolving landscape of global transportation networks.

Strategies for Long-Term Success:

The book concludes by offering strategic insights for long-term success in transportation investments. This includes the importance of diversification, adaptation to technological changes, and the incorporation of sustainable and responsible investment practices.

In essence, "Navigating Wealth" is designed to be a comprehensive and practical resource, guiding readers through the intricate world of transportation investments, fostering a deeper understanding of the sector, and empowering individuals and entities to contribute to the development of sustainable and prosperous transportation networks.

Chapter II: Understanding the Transportation Landscape

A. Overview of the Global Transportation Industry:

The global transportation industry serves as the intricate circulatory system that fuels the interconnected economies of the world. From bustling urban centers to remote corners of the globe, the movement of people and goods is facilitated by a diverse array of transportation modes. This section aims to provide a comprehensive overview of the global transportation industry, offering insights into its various components, economic significance, and pivotal role in shaping societies.

1. Modes of Transportation:

The global transportation industry encompasses a multitude of modes that collectively form a complex and dynamic network:

Road Networks: Covering the vast expanse of highways, streets, and thoroughfares, road networks are the backbone of local and regional transportation, supporting the movement of goods and people.

Railways: Rail transport, with its efficiency and capacity for heavy cargo, plays a vital role in both freight and passenger transportation, connecting cities and countries across vast landmasses.

Aviation: Air travel, facilitated by a network of airports and airlines, provides rapid and efficient connectivity on a global scale, fostering international trade and enabling swift movement of people.

Maritime Shipping: Seaborne trade is facilitated by a vast network of ports and shipping routes, connecting continents and enabling the movement of goods on a massive scale.

Mass Transit Systems: In urban environments, mass transit systems such as buses, subways, and light rail contribute to efficient intra-city transportation, alleviating congestion and reducing environmental impact.

2. Interconnected Networks:

The seamless interconnectivity of these transportation modes forms the foundation of a global transportation ecosystem. Multimodal transportation, where goods and people smoothly transition from one mode to another, enhances the overall efficiency of the transportation network.

Intermodal Hubs: Key locations, such as ports and logistics hubs, serve as intermodal hubs where different modes of transportation converge, facilitating the transfer of cargo and streamlining supply chains.

3. Economic Contribution:

The economic impact of the transportation industry reverberates across nations and industries:

Job Creation: The industry generates employment at various levels, from logistics and infrastructure development to operational roles in airlines, shipping companies, and public transportation.

Trade Facilitation: Efficient transportation systems reduce trade barriers, fostering global commerce and enabling nations to participate in the international marketplace.

Investment and Infrastructure Development: The industry attracts substantial investments in the development and maintenance of transportation infrastructure, driving economic growth and enhancing connectivity.

This comprehensive overview sets the stage for a deeper exploration of the global transportation landscape, laying the groundwork for understanding the intricacies of each mode, the challenges faced by the industry, and the opportunities for strategic investments explored in subsequent chapters.

B. Key Players and Stakeholders:

Understanding the global transportation industry requires recognizing the diverse array of players and stakeholders who contribute to its development, operation, and regulation. This section identifies and explores the roles of key players and stakeholders, ranging from government entities to private sector organizations and technology innovators.

1. Government Agencies and Authorities:

Government bodies play a central role in regulating, overseeing, and shaping the transportation landscape:

Transportation Departments: National and regional transportation departments formulate policies, set regulatory frameworks, and oversee the planning and development of transportation infrastructure.

Regulatory Authorities: Entities such as the Federal Aviation Administration (FAA), International Maritime Organization (IMO), and others set industry standards, ensuring safety, security, and compliance with international regulations.

2. Private Sector Entities:

Private companies and organizations contribute significantly to the functioning and evolution of the transportation industry:

Logistics and Shipping Companies: Entities involved in the movement of goods, managing supply chains, and operating shipping services contribute to the efficiency of global trade.

Airlines: Commercial airlines provide passenger and cargo services, connecting cities and countries across the globe. Both legacy carriers and low-cost airlines play crucial roles.

Railway Operators: Companies managing railway systems are pivotal in both freight and passenger transportation, especially in regions with extensive rail networks.

Infrastructure Developers: Private entities engaged in the planning, construction, and maintenance of transportation infrastructure, including roads, airports, and ports.

Technology Providers: Companies specializing in transportation technology contribute to innovations such as intelligent transportation systems, digital platforms, and advancements in vehicle design.

3. Technology Providers:

The integration of technology is transforming the transportation industry:

Automotive and Vehicle Manufacturers: Companies producing automobiles, electric vehicles, and autonomous vehicles are at the forefront of shaping the future of personal and freight transportation.

Tech Innovators: Technology companies developing solutions for smart transportation, including IoT applications, artificial intelligence, and data analytics that enhance efficiency and safety.

4. Consumers and End Users:

Individuals and businesses that rely on transportation services are critical stakeholders:

Consumers: Individuals using transportation services for personal travel, and businesses relying on efficient logistics and supply chain solutions.

Industries Dependent on Transport: Sectors such as manufacturing, retail, and agriculture, whose operations hinge on the reliable movement of goods.

5. Financial Institutions and Investors:

Entities providing capital and investment play a crucial role in shaping the trajectory of transportation infrastructure:

Banks and Financial Institutions: Providing loans and financial instruments to fund transportation projects, including infrastructure development and equipment acquisition.

Private Investors: Individuals, investment funds, and private equity firms contributing capital to transportation projects and initiatives.

Understanding the roles and interactions of these key players and stakeholders is vital for comprehending the dynamics of the global transportation industry. As the industry continues to evolve, the collaboration and coordination among these entities will shape the future landscape of transportation.

C. Trends and Innovations in Transportation:

The landscape of global transportation is continuously evolving, driven by technological advancements, changing consumer behaviors, and a growing emphasis on sustainability. This section explores key trends and innovations that are reshaping the industry, influencing the way people and goods move, and paving the way for a more connected and efficient future.

1. Digital Transformation and Intelligent Transportation Systems:

Smart Infrastructure: The integration of sensors, IoT devices, and data analytics into transportation infrastructure is creating smart cities with intelligent traffic management, dynamic signaling, and real-time information for commuters.

Connected Vehicles: The rise of connected vehicles, equipped with advanced communication systems, enables real-time data sharing between vehicles and infrastructure, improving traffic flow, reducing congestion, and enhancing safety.

2. Sustainable and Green Transportation:

Electric Vehicles (EVs): The transition to electric vehicles is a prominent trend, driven by environmental concerns and advancements in battery technology. Governments and industries are investing in EV infrastructure to support this shift.

Public Transit Electrification: The electrification of public transit systems, including buses and trains, contributes to reducing carbon emissions and creating more sustainable urban transportation options.

Alternative Fuels: Exploration of alternative fuels, such as hydrogen and biofuels, as viable options to reduce the carbon footprint of traditional transportation modes.

3. Autonomous and Connected Vehicles:

Autonomous Vehicles (AVs): The development and testing of autonomous vehicles, ranging from self-driving cars to trucks, with potential implications for safety, efficiency, and the redesign of transportation systems.

Connected Fleets: The connectivity of commercial vehicle fleets for real-time tracking, predictive maintenance, and route optimization, enhancing overall efficiency and reducing operational costs.

4. Urban Mobility Solutions:

Micro-Mobility: The emergence of micro-mobility solutions, including electric scooters and bike-sharing programs, as alternative modes of transportation for short distances within urban areas.

Mobility as a Service (MaaS): The integration of various transportation services into a unified, seamless platform, allowing users to plan, book, and pay for multi-modal journeys using a single app.

5. Globalization and Trade Routes:

New Trade Routes: The development of new trade routes and corridors, often facilitated by mega infrastructure projects, influencing global trade patterns and creating opportunities for strategic investments.

E-commerce Impact: The growth of e-commerce has led to increased demand for efficient and rapid last-mile delivery solutions, prompting innovations in logistics and supply chain management.

6. Resilience and Safety Innovations:

Emergency Response Systems: Integration of advanced communication systems and predictive analytics to enhance emergency response systems, improving safety measures and reducing response times in case of accidents or disasters.

Cybersecurity in Transportation: The rising importance of cybersecurity measures to protect transportation systems from potential threats and ensure the integrity of connected and autonomous vehicles.

Exploring these trends and innovations provides a forward-looking perspective on the future of transportation. As the industry continues to adapt to these changes, strategic investors and stakeholders can position themselves to leverage opportunities and contribute to the development of a more sustainable, efficient, and interconnected global transportation network.

Chapter III: Types of Transport Investments

A. Traditional Investments

1. Road Infrastructure:

Overview: Road infrastructure investments constitute the construction, maintenance, and improvement of road networks. This includes highways, expressways, bridges, tunnels, and urban road systems.

Economic Impact: Well-developed roads reduce travel times, enhance accessibility, and lower transportation costs. They play a crucial role in economic development by facilitating the movement of goods, connecting regions, and supporting industries.

Examples of Investments:

Expansion and widening of highways.

Bridge and tunnel construction projects.

Urban road rehabilitation and modernization initiatives.

2. Rail and Mass Transit Systems:

Overview: Investments in rail and mass transit systems involve the development and improvement of both freight and passenger rail networks. This includes national and regional railways, metro systems, light rail, and high-speed rail projects.

Economic Impact: Efficient rail and mass transit systems reduce congestion, lower emissions, and provide sustainable urban transportation solutions. They contribute to economic growth by supporting the movement of people and goods.

Examples of Investments:

High-speed rail projects connecting major cities.

Expansion and modernization of metro and light rail systems.

Freight rail network upgrades for efficient cargo transport.

3. Airports and Aviation:

Overview: Investments in airports and aviation infrastructure focus on the expansion, modernization, and improvement of airports. This includes runway upgrades, terminal developments, and technology enhancements.

Economic Impact: Upgraded airports enhance global connectivity, stimulate tourism, and support various industries dependent on air transportation. They play a critical role in facilitating international trade.

Examples of Investments:

Construction of new airport terminals.

Runway extensions and improvements.

Implementation of advanced air traffic control systems.

4. Maritime and Ports:

Overview: Investments in maritime infrastructure center around the development and expansion of ports and shipping facilities. This includes dredging projects, container terminal expansions, and improved navigational channels.

Economic Impact: Efficient ports contribute to economic competitiveness by facilitating the movement of goods, reducing shipping costs, and supporting international trade.

Examples of Investments:

Expansion of container terminals.

Dredging projects to accommodate larger vessels.

Upgrades to port facilities for enhanced cargo handling.

Traditional investments in road, rail, aviation, and maritime infrastructure are fundamental to the functioning of global transportation systems. They not only improve connectivity but also play a pivotal role in fostering economic development, job creation, and sustainable growth. Understanding the nuances of these investments is crucial for stakeholders aiming to navigate the complexities of the traditional transportation landscape.

B. Emerging Opportunities

1. Sustainable Transportation:

Overview: Sustainable transportation investments focus on environmentally friendly modes of mobility, aiming to reduce the carbon footprint and promote eco-conscious practices. This includes the development of public transit systems, cycling infrastructure, and pedestrian-friendly urban planning.

Economic Impact: Sustainable transportation investments contribute to cleaner air, reduced traffic congestion, and improved quality of life in urban areas. They align with the growing demand for eco-friendly solutions in the transportation sector.

Examples of Investments:

Implementation of bike-sharing programs.

Development of electric bus fleets.

Creation of pedestrian zones and green transport corridors.

2. Electric and Autonomous Vehicles:

Overview: Investments in electric and autonomous vehicles represent a transformative shift in personal and freight transportation. Electric vehicles aim to reduce dependence on fossil fuels, while autonomous vehicles offer the potential for safer and more efficient travel.

Economic Impact: The development and adoption of electric and autonomous vehicles can revolutionize the automotive industry, reduce environmental impact, and reshape transportation systems.

Examples of Investments:

Construction of electric vehicle charging infrastructure.

Research and development in autonomous vehicle technologies.

Implementation of autonomous vehicle testing programs.

3. High-Speed Rail and Hyperloop:

Overview: High-speed rail and hyperloop investments aim to revolutionize long-distance travel by significantly reducing travel times. High-speed rail projects focus on upgrading rail networks for faster passenger and freight transport, while hyperloop envisions ultra-fast, tube-based transportation.

Economic Impact: These projects can stimulate economic growth, create jobs, and provide more efficient alternatives to traditional transportation modes.

Examples of Investments:

Construction of high-speed rail networks connecting major cities.

Research and feasibility studies for hyperloop transportation systems.

Implementation of high-speed rail projects to enhance regional connectivity.

4. Drone Delivery Systems:

Overview: Investments in drone delivery systems explore the use of unmanned aerial vehicles for transporting goods. This emerging opportunity has the potential to revolutionize last-mile delivery in remote or challenging terrains.

Economic Impact: Drone delivery systems can enhance logistics efficiency, reduce last-mile delivery costs, and provide faster and more flexible delivery options.

Examples of Investments:

Development of drone technology for package delivery.

Regulatory frameworks to enable safe and widespread drone use in logistics.

Implementation of drone delivery pilot programs.

Emerging opportunities in sustainable transportation, electric and autonomous vehicles, high-speed rail, hyperloop, and drone delivery systems represent the frontier of innovation in the transportation sector. These investments not only address environmental concerns but also open new avenues for efficient, fast, and sustainable transportation solutions in the 21st century. Understanding these opportunities is crucial for stakeholders looking to invest strategically and shape the future of transportation.

Chapter IV: Risk Analysis and Mitigation Strategies

A. Economic and Regulatory Risks:

1. Economic Risks:

Overview: Economic factors play a significant role in shaping the success of transportation investments. Economic risks encompass a range of uncertainties that can impact the financial performance and viability of projects.

Mitigation Strategies:

Diversification of Investments: Spread investments across diverse projects and sectors to minimize exposure to economic downturns in a specific area.

Thorough Market Research: Conduct comprehensive market analyses to anticipate economic trends and identify potential risks early on.

Flexible Financial Models: Develop financial models that can adapt to changing economic conditions, incorporating sensitivity analyses and stress testing.

2. Regulatory Risks:

Overview: The regulatory environment is dynamic, and changes in regulations can significantly affect the operation and profitability of transportation projects. Regulatory risks include shifts in policies, tariffs, and safety standards.

Mitigation Strategies:

Regular Engagement with Regulatory Authorities: Maintain open communication with relevant regulatory bodies to stay informed about potential changes and provide input during regulatory discussions.

Stay Informed: Establish mechanisms to stay updated on regulatory developments, including subscribing to industry publications and participating in industry forums.

Build Flexibility into Project Plans: Design projects with flexibility to accommodate changes in regulations, ensuring adaptability to evolving compliance requirements.

Navigating economic and regulatory risks requires a proactive and informed approach. By anticipating potential challenges and implementing mitigation strategies, stakeholders can enhance the resilience of transportation investments in the face of economic uncertainties and regulatory changes.

B. Technological and Innovation Risks:

1. Technological Risks:

Overview: The rapid pace of technological advancements introduces the risk of existing technologies becoming obsolete or facing unexpected challenges during implementation.

Mitigation Strategies:

Continuous Monitoring: Stay abreast of technological developments through regular monitoring of industry trends, research publications, and collaboration with technology experts.

Invest in Adaptable Technologies: Prioritize technologies that offer scalability and adaptability to evolving industry standards and emerging innovations.

Incorporate Scalability: Design projects with scalability in mind, enabling the integration of new technologies without significant disruptions to existing systems.

2. Innovation Risks:

Overview: Investments in innovative technologies, such as autonomous vehicles or hyperloop systems, come with uncertainties and potential challenges during development and implementation.

Mitigation Strategies:

Rigorous Testing: Conduct extensive testing and pilot projects to validate the functionality, safety, and reliability of innovative technologies before full-scale implementation.

Collaboration with Research Institutions: Foster collaborations with research institutions and industry experts to leverage their expertise and insights during the development and deployment of innovative solutions.

Maintain Flexibility: Acknowledge that innovation projects may encounter unforeseen hurdles and delays; maintain flexibility in project timelines and budgets to accommodate unexpected challenges.

Navigating technological and innovation risks requires a strategic and adaptive approach. By staying informed about technological advancements, prioritizing adaptable solutions, and embracing a culture of innovation and flexibility, stakeholders can position themselves to harness the benefits of cutting-edge technologies while mitigating potential risks.

C. Environmental and Social Impact Assessment:
1. Environmental Risks:

Overview: Transport projects can have environmental implications, including habitat disruption, pollution, and resource depletion, which may lead to regulatory scrutiny and public opposition.

Mitigation Strategies:

Comprehensive Environmental Impact Assessments (EIA): Conduct thorough EIAs to identify potential environmental impacts, assess risks, and develop mitigation plans.

Sustainable Practices: Implement sustainable construction and operational practices to minimize environmental footprints, including the use of eco-friendly materials and energy-efficient technologies.

Adherence to Regulations: Ensure strict compliance with environmental regulations and standards, collaborating with environmental authorities to address concerns.

2. Social Impact Risks:

Overview: Transport projects can affect local communities, leading to issues such as displacement, changes in living conditions, and disruptions to local economies.

Mitigation Strategies:

Community Engagement: Engage with local communities throughout the project lifecycle to understand their concerns, gather feedback, and build positive relationships.

Social Impact Assessments (SIA): Conduct SIAs to evaluate potential social impacts, identify vulnerable populations, and develop strategies to mitigate negative effects.

Community Development Programs: Implement community development initiatives to enhance local infrastructure, education, and employment opportunities, fostering positive social outcomes.

Navigating environmental and social impact risks involves a commitment to responsible and sustainable practices. By conducting thorough assessments, adhering to regulations, and actively engaging with local communities, stakeholders can contribute to projects that not only meet economic objectives but also align with environmental and social responsibility.

D. Legal and Political Considerations:
1. Legal Risks:

Overview: Legal challenges, including disputes over land acquisition, contractual obligations, and regulatory compliance, can pose significant risks to transport investments.

Mitigation Strategies:

Thorough Legal Due Diligence: Conduct comprehensive legal due diligence before initiating projects to identify potential legal risks and liabilities.

Clear Contractual Agreements: Develop well-defined and legally sound contractual agreements with all involved parties to minimize the risk of disputes.

Alternative Dispute Resolution (ADR): Include provisions for alternative dispute resolution mechanisms, such as arbitration or mediation, to expedite conflict resolution.

2. Political Risks:
Overview: Political instability, changes in government, and geopolitical tensions can impact the stability and success of transport investments.

Mitigation Strategies:
Diversification of Investments: Spread investments across different regions and countries to mitigate the impact of political instability in a specific area.

Stay Informed about Geopolitical Developments: Regularly monitor geopolitical developments and maintain awareness of political risks that may impact the investment landscape.

Build Relationships with Political Stakeholders: Establish strong relationships with local and national political stakeholders to navigate political landscapes effectively.

Navigating legal and political considerations is essential for the success and sustainability of transport investments. By incorporating thorough legal due diligence, establishing clear contractual agreements, and staying informed about geopolitical developments, stakeholders can better manage the complexities associated with legal and political risks.

Chapter V: Case Studies

A. Successful Transport Investments

Transport investments that demonstrate success often share common characteristics, including strategic planning, effective execution, and positive impacts on economic, social, and environmental aspects. The following case studies highlight instances where transport investments have yielded significant positive outcomes:

1. High-Return Road Infrastructure Projects:

Case Study: XYZ Expressway Expansion

Overview:

The XYZ Expressway Expansion project aimed to enhance regional connectivity through the development of an extensive road network. The project included the construction of additional lanes, modernized toll booths, and improved traffic management systems.

Key Success Factors:

Thorough Feasibility Studies: Extensive studies were conducted to analyze traffic patterns, assess economic benefits, and identify potential challenges. This informed decision-making and ensured the project's viability.

Public-Private Partnership (PPP): The project adopted a successful PPP model, engaging private sector participation in financing, construction, and operation. This collaborative approach shared both risks and returns effectively.

Outcomes:

Reduced Travel Times: The expanded expressway significantly reduced travel times between major cities, enhancing regional accessibility.

Economic Growth: Increased economic activities in the connected regions, leading to job creation and business development.

High Return on Investment: Toll revenues exceeded projections, providing a substantial return on investment for both public and private stakeholders.

2. Transformative Mass Transit Systems:

Case Study: City X Bus Rapid Transit (BRT) System

Overview:

City X implemented a transformative Bus Rapid Transit (BRT) system to address urban congestion and provide a sustainable public transit solution. The BRT system featured dedicated lanes, efficient station placement, and integrated technologies for streamlined operations.

Key Success Factors:

Effective Planning and Design: The BRT system was strategically planned, optimizing routes, station locations, and connectivity with other modes of transportation.

Public Engagement: Stakeholder engagement, including public input and community outreach, ensured the project aligned with community needs and garnered public support.

Outcomes:

Reduced Congestion: The BRT system significantly reduced traffic congestion, providing a faster and more efficient alternative to private transport.

Increased Ridership: A surge in public transportation usage indicated the success of the BRT system in meeting the needs of the urban population.

Improved Air Quality: With fewer vehicles on the road, the BRT system contributed to improved air quality and environmental sustainability.

3. Sustainable Transport Initiatives:

Case Study: City Y Electric Bike-Sharing Program

Overview:

City Y introduced an electric bike-sharing program to promote sustainable urban mobility. The program provided residents with convenient and eco-friendly transportation options, contributing to the city's environmental goals.

Key Success Factors:

Integration of Technology: A user-friendly mobile app facilitated easy bike rentals, payments, and real-time tracking, enhancing user experience.

Collaboration with Stakeholders: The initiative involved collaboration with local businesses, city authorities, and environmental groups to create a unified approach toward sustainability.

Outcomes:

Reduced Carbon Emissions: The electric bike-sharing program contributed to a significant reduction in carbon emissions, aligning with the city's environmental objectives.

Eased Traffic Congestion: The program provided a sustainable alternative for short-distance travel, contributing to reduced traffic congestion.

Positive Public Reception: The initiative gained popularity among residents, reflecting a positive response to sustainable transport options.

These case studies exemplify successful transport investments that have not only improved infrastructure but also contributed to economic growth, environmental sustainability, and enhanced quality of life for residents. They highlight the importance of strategic planning, stakeholder engagement, and innovative approaches in achieving positive outcomes in the transportation sector.

B. Lessons from Failed Investments

Understanding the challenges and shortcomings of failed transport investments is crucial for refining future strategies, mitigating risks, and improving decision-making processes. The following case studies explore the lessons learned from unsuccessful transport investments:

1. Regulatory Challenges:

Case Study: Cross-Border Railway Project

Overview:

A major cross-border railway project faced prolonged delays and eventual failure due to regulatory disputes between neighboring countries. Inconsistent regulations regarding land acquisition, safety standards, and operational protocols led to insurmountable challenges.

Key Lessons:

Early Regulatory Assessment: A thorough analysis of cross-border regulatory frameworks and coordination between involved governments is essential before initiating large-scale projects.

Legal Contingencies: Projects should incorporate legal contingencies and dispute resolution mechanisms to address potential regulatory challenges and prevent lengthy delays.

2. Technological Setbacks:

Case Study: Autonomous Vehicle Fleet Project

Overview:

The development of an autonomous vehicle fleet faced setbacks due to technology malfunctions and insufficient testing. Safety concerns and public skepticism led to the project's failure.

Key Lessons:

Rigorous Testing Protocols: Extensive testing phases, including simulated and real-world scenarios, are crucial to identify and address potential technological issues before widespread implementation.

Public Awareness and Acceptance: Proactive engagement with the public is necessary to build awareness and acceptance of new technologies, addressing concerns and expectations.

3. Economic and Political Factors:

Case Study: Abandoned High-Speed Rail Project

Overview:

An ambitious high-speed rail project faced financial challenges during an economic recession. Changing political priorities led to reduced government support, ultimately resulting in the project's abandonment.

Key Lessons:

Risk Mitigation Strategies: Develop robust risk mitigation strategies that account for potential economic downturns and political shifts.

Stakeholder Alignment: Ensure alignment with political stakeholders and secure long-term financial commitments to weather economic uncertainties.

Learning from failed transport investments emphasizes the importance of comprehensive planning, risk mitigation, and adaptability. These case studies underscore the need for careful consideration of regulatory landscapes, robust testing protocols for innovative technologies, and a thorough understanding of economic and political factors to navigate challenges effectively. By incorporating these lessons into future projects, stakeholders can enhance the likelihood of success and sustainability in the dynamic field of transportation investments.

Chapter VI: Financial Modeling and Analysis

A. Cost-Benefit Analysis:

Overview:

Cost-Benefit Analysis (CBA) is a systematic approach used to evaluate the economic feasibility of transport investments by comparing the costs and benefits associated with a project. This analysis provides a comprehensive framework for decision-making, helping stakeholders assess the potential impact of a project on the economy, society, and the environment.

Key Components:

Identification of Costs and Benefits:

Direct Costs: Tangible expenses directly related to the project, such as construction costs, land acquisition, and operational expenses.

Indirect Costs: Intangible expenses that may impact the project, including environmental and social costs.

Monetization of Impacts:

Assigning monetary values to both costs and benefits to facilitate a quantitative comparison.

Considering factors like time, resources, and environmental impact during the monetization process.

Discounting:

Adjusting future costs and benefits to present value to account for the time value of money.

Applying a discount rate to reflect the opportunity cost of using resources today rather than in the future.

Sensitivity Analysis:

Assessing the impact of variations in key variables on the overall cost-benefit ratio.

Identifying the sensitivity of the analysis to changes in factors such as project duration, interest rates, or benefit estimations.

Importance:

Informs Decision-Making:

Provides a structured approach for comparing alternative projects and making informed investment decisions.

Enables stakeholders to weigh the economic, social, and environmental implications of a project.

Facilitates Stakeholder Communication:

Translates complex financial data into a format accessible to various stakeholders.

Enhances transparency and communication by presenting a clear picture of the project's potential impacts and trade-offs.

Challenges:

Subjectivity in Monetization:

Assigning monetary values to intangible benefits or costs may involve subjective judgments.

Stakeholder consensus and transparency are essential to address these subjective elements.

Difficulty in Predicting Future Impacts:

Predicting future benefits and costs accurately can be challenging, especially in long-term projects.

Regular reviews and adjustments to the analysis can address evolving conditions and uncertainties.

Cost-Benefit Analysis is a fundamental tool in the decision-making process for transport investments. By carefully identifying, monetizing, and discounting costs and benefits, stakeholders can gain valuable insights into the potential impact of a project, aiding in the selection of economically sound and socially responsible transportation initiatives.

B. Return on Investment (ROI) Calculation:

Overview:

Return on Investment (ROI) is a critical financial metric used to evaluate the profitability and efficiency of a transport investment. It measures the ratio of net gains to the initial investment, providing stakeholders with a percentage-based indicator of the project's financial performance.

Calculation Formula:

ROI=NetGain / InitialInvestment*100

Key Components:

Net Gain Calculation:

Subtracting the total costs from the total benefits to determine the net gain.

Accounting for both tangible and intangible gains and losses associated with the project.

Time Frame:

Determining the appropriate time frame for measuring returns, considering project duration and the nature of benefits (short-term vs. long-term).

Aligning the time frame with the project's objectives and expected lifecycle.

Risk Adjustment:

Considering risk factors and uncertainties in ROI calculations to provide a more realistic assessment.

Incorporating a risk premium or sensitivity analysis to account for potential variations in key variables.

Importance:

Evaluates Profitability:

Assesses the efficiency of the investment in generating returns over time.

Provides a straightforward metric for comparing different projects and investment opportunities.

Decision Support:

Guides decision-makers in selecting projects with the highest potential for returns.

Facilitates the comparison of alternative investments, supporting informed decision-making.

Challenges:

Complexity in Net Gain Calculation:

Determining and quantifying all relevant costs and benefits can be complex, especially for long-term projects.

Thorough documentation and collaboration with subject matter experts are essential to address this challenge.

Subjectivity in Risk Assessment:

Assessing and adjusting for risks involves subjective judgment, and different stakeholders may have varying risk tolerances.

Open communication and collaboration among stakeholders are crucial for aligning risk assessments.

Considerations for Stakeholders:

Holistic View of Gains and Losses:

Consider both direct financial gains and broader, indirect impacts on stakeholders, communities, and the environment.

Regular Review and Adjustment:

Periodically review and adjust ROI calculations, especially for long-term projects, to account for changing conditions and uncertainties.

Return on Investment is a key financial metric that provides a clear indication of a project's financial success. By accurately calculating ROI, stakeholders can make informed decisions, allocate resources efficiently, and prioritize projects with the greatest potential for positive returns in the transportation sector.

C. Financing Options and Public-Private Partnerships (PPPs):
Overview:

Financing is a critical aspect of successful transport projects, and exploring various options, including Public-Private Partnerships (PPPs), is essential for securing the necessary capital. This chapter delves into different financing avenues and the collaborative approach of PPPs in the context of transportation investments.

Key Components:
Debt Financing:

Description: Obtaining loans or issuing bonds to raise capital for the project.

Considerations: Interest rates, repayment terms, and the ability to service the debt from project revenues.

Equity Financing:

Description: Attracting investors who contribute capital in exchange for a share of ownership or profits.

Considerations: Equity structure, dividend distribution, and the alignment of investor interests with project success.

Public-Private Partnerships (PPPs):

Description: Collaborative arrangements between public and private entities to finance, design, build, operate, and maintain infrastructure projects.

Key Models:

Build-Operate-Transfer (BOT): Private entity designs, builds, and operates the project for a specified period before transferring it to the public sector.

Design-Build-Finance-Operate (DBFO): Private entity assumes responsibility for design, construction, financing, and operation.

Importance:
Risk Allocation:

PPPs allow the allocation of risks to the party best equipped to manage them, improving overall risk management.

Risks may include construction delays, cost overruns, and revenue fluctuations.

Innovative Financing Models:

Explore innovative financing models to leverage private sector expertise and capital.

BOT and DBFO models allow private entities to bring innovation and efficiency to project execution.

Sustainability:

Choose financing options that align with the project's long-term sustainability and financial health.

Balance debt and equity components to ensure the project's ability to meet financial obligations.

Challenges:

Complexity of PPP Arrangements:

PPPs involve complex contractual agreements and negotiations, requiring a thorough understanding of legal, financial, and operational aspects.

Engage legal and financial experts to navigate the intricacies of PPP structures.

Political and Public Perception:

Public perception and political support can influence the success of PPPs.

Proactive communication, transparency, and stakeholder engagement are crucial for building trust.

Considerations for Stakeholders:

Diversification of Financing Sources:

Consider a mix of debt and equity financing to diversify funding sources and mitigate financial risks.

Evaluate the cost of capital and the impact on project viability.

Long-Term Financial Viability:

Assess the long-term financial viability of the project, considering revenue streams, operating costs, and potential economic shifts.

Establish mechanisms for periodic financial reviews and adjustments.

Stakeholder Engagement:

Engage with stakeholders, including the public, to build understanding and support for financing mechanisms.

Address concerns and communicate the potential benefits of the chosen financing approach.

Financing options and PPPs play a pivotal role in bringing transportation projects to fruition. By carefully evaluating debt and equity structures and navigating the complexities of PPP arrangements, stakeholders can secure the necessary resources and drive the successful implementation of transformative transport initiatives.

Chapter VII: Future Trends and Opportunities

A. Anticipated Developments in Transportation:

Overview:

Anticipating future developments in transportation is essential for stakeholders to proactively align their strategies with emerging trends and opportunities. This section explores key areas expected to shape the future of transportation.

1. Sustainable Mobility:

Trend: The transportation industry is undergoing a paradigm shift towards sustainability, emphasizing eco-friendly modes of travel.

Opportunity: Investments in sustainable mobility initiatives, such as electric vehicles, bike-sharing programs, and enhanced public transit systems, present opportunities to align with environmental goals and meet the rising demand for eco-conscious transportation options. This includes exploring advancements in energy-efficient technologies and alternative fuels.

2. Urban Air Mobility (UAM):

Trend: Advances in vertical takeoff and landing (VTOL) technologies are opening new possibilities for urban air mobility, including the development of flying taxis and autonomous aerial vehicles.

Opportunity: Stakeholders can explore investments in UAM infrastructure and technology to position themselves at the forefront of this transformative trend. This includes considerations for airspace management, vertiports, and regulatory frameworks to support the integration of aerial mobility into urban landscapes.

3. Hyperloop and High-Speed Rail:

Trend: Ongoing development of high-speed rail and hyperloop technologies aims to revolutionize long-distance travel with rapid, efficient, and sustainable transportation systems.

Opportunity: Investing in the infrastructure and technology required for high-speed rail and hyperloop systems provides opportunities to enhance regional and inter-city connectivity. This involves collaboration with technology developers, policymakers, and regional authorities to bring these innovations to fruition.

4. Mobility as a Service (MaaS):

Trend: The emergence of Mobility as a Service (MaaS) platforms, integrating various transportation services into a unified, user-centric experience.

Opportunity: Investments in MaaS platforms and technologies can streamline transportation for users, offering integrated solutions for different modes of transport. This includes partnerships with technology providers, data analytics companies, and service operators to create seamless and convenient mobility options.

5. Smart Infrastructure and Connectivity:

Trend: The integration of smart technologies into transportation infrastructure, including connected vehicles, smart traffic management, and real-time data analytics.

Opportunity: Investing in smart infrastructure provides opportunities to enhance safety, efficiency, and sustainability. Stakeholders can explore partnerships with technology providers, data analytics firms, and governmental bodies to contribute to the development of intelligent transportation systems.

6. Advanced Materials and Sustainable Infrastructure:

Trend: Advances in materials science leading to the development of sustainable and durable infrastructure components.

Opportunity: Investments in innovative materials and construction technologies contribute to the development of resilient and eco-friendly transportation infrastructure. This includes exploring partnerships with research institutions and industry leaders to implement cutting-edge materials in construction projects.

Anticipating these developments allows stakeholders to position themselves strategically in the evolving landscape of transportation. By embracing sustainability, exploring emerging technologies, and actively participating in transformative trends, stakeholders can contribute to the development of a future-ready and resilient transportation ecosystem.

B. Technological Advancements Shaping the Industry:

Overview:

The rapid evolution of technology is a driving force in shaping the future of the transportation industry. Stakeholders need to be cognizant of these advancements to remain competitive and meet the evolving demands of passengers and cargo transport.

1. Autonomous Vehicles:

Advancement: The continued development and deployment of autonomous vehicles for both passenger and freight transport.

Impact: Autonomous vehicles have the potential to enhance safety, increase efficiency, and reduce the need for human intervention in transportation systems. Stakeholders should consider the integration of autonomous technologies into their fleets and infrastructure.

2. Internet of Things (IoT) Integration:

Advancement: The integration of IoT technologies for real-time data collection, monitoring, and communication in transportation systems.

Impact: The use of IoT enables real-time insights into traffic patterns, vehicle health, and infrastructure conditions. This enhances traffic management, enables predictive maintenance, and improves overall system efficiency. Stakeholders should explore IoT applications to optimize their operations.

3. Advanced Traffic Management Systems:

Advancement: Implementation of advanced traffic management systems using artificial intelligence (AI) and data analytics.

Impact: AI-powered traffic management systems can analyze vast amounts of data to optimize traffic flow, reduce congestion, and enhance safety. Stakeholders should invest in and collaborate with technology providers to implement cutting-edge traffic management solutions.

4. Electric and Hybrid Vehicles:

Advancement: The ongoing development and adoption of electric and hybrid vehicles for sustainable transportation.

Impact: The shift towards electric and hybrid vehicles contributes to reducing carbon emissions and reliance on traditional fuels. Stakeholders, including manufacturers and infrastructure providers, should align their strategies with the growing demand for sustainable transportation solutions.

5. Hyperloop and Maglev Technologies:

Advancement: Advancements in hyperloop and maglev technologies for high-speed, energy-efficient transportation.

Impact: These technologies offer the potential for rapid and efficient inter-city travel. Stakeholders should explore partnerships and investments in the development of hyperloop and maglev infrastructure to enhance long-distance connectivity.

6. Blockchain for Logistics and Supply Chain:

Advancement: The application of blockchain technology for secure and transparent logistics and supply chain management.

Impact: Blockchain enhances transparency, traceability, and security in the movement of goods. Stakeholders in logistics and transportation should explore blockchain applications to optimize supply chain processes and build trust among participants.

7. Augmented Reality (AR) for Navigation:

Advancement: The integration of augmented reality (AR) technologies for enhanced navigation and driver assistance.

Impact: AR provides real-time information and guidance to drivers, improving navigation and safety. Stakeholders in automotive and technology sectors should explore AR applications to enhance user experiences and safety features.

Understanding and leveraging these technological advancements is crucial for stakeholders to remain at the forefront of the evolving transportation landscape. By adopting and investing in these technologies, stakeholders can enhance efficiency, sustainability, and safety in the transportation industry.

C. Policy and Regulatory Influences on Future Investments:
Overview:
Government policies and regulations play a pivotal role in shaping the trajectory of transportation investments. Understanding and adapting to these influences is crucial for stakeholders to navigate the regulatory landscape effectively and align their strategies with future developments.

1. Sustainable and Smart Cities Initiatives:

Policy Influence: Increasing focus on sustainable and smart city initiatives to enhance urban living and transportation.

Impact: Opportunities for investments in smart infrastructure, intelligent transportation systems, and sustainable mobility solutions. Stakeholders should align their projects with city development plans and seek partnerships with municipal authorities.

2. Electrification and Emission Standards:
Policy Influence: Stringent emission standards and incentives for the electrification of transport.

Impact: Drives investments in electric vehicles, charging infrastructure, and sustainable transportation alternatives. Stakeholders should align their strategies with evolving emission standards and explore opportunities in the electric vehicle market.

3. Public-Private Collaboration Initiatives:
Policy Influence: Encouragement of public-private collaborations to drive innovation and investment in transportation.

Impact: Opportunities for private sector involvement in infrastructure development, technology implementation, and service delivery. Stakeholders should actively seek partnerships with government agencies to contribute to transportation advancements.

4. Intelligent Transportation Systems (ITS) Mandates:

Policy Influence: Mandates for the implementation of Intelligent Transportation Systems (ITS) for improved traffic management and safety.

Impact: Drives investments in technology solutions for real-time data collection, traffic analysis, and safety enhancements. Stakeholders should align their projects with ITS requirements and invest in technologies that contribute to safer and more efficient transportation.

5. Urban Planning and Zoning Regulations:

Policy Influence: Integration of transportation considerations into urban planning and zoning regulations.

Impact: Influences the design of transportation infrastructure and the development of transit-oriented spaces. Stakeholders should collaborate with urban planners and policymakers to ensure that transportation investments align with broader city planning goals.

6. Data Privacy and Cybersecurity Regulations:

Policy Influence: Increasing focus on data privacy and cybersecurity regulations, particularly in the context of connected vehicles and smart infrastructure.

Impact: Requires investments in secure and compliant technologies to protect user data and ensure the cybersecurity of transportation systems. Stakeholders should prioritize cybersecurity measures and compliance with data protection regulations.

7. Funding Allocations and Grants:

Policy Influence: Governmental funding allocations and grants to support specific types of transportation projects.

Impact: Provides financial support and incentives for targeted projects, influencing investment priorities. Stakeholders should stay informed about funding opportunities and align their projects with government priorities to access available grants.

Understanding the policy and regulatory landscape is essential for successful transportation investments. Stakeholders should actively engage with policymakers, monitor regulatory developments, and adapt their strategies to align with evolving government priorities and mandates. This proactive approach ensures that investments are not only financially sound but also compliant with the regulatory framework.

Chapter VIII: Strategies for Long-Term Success

A. Diversification of Transport Investments:

Overview:

Diversification is a fundamental strategy for building a resilient and sustainable portfolio in the realm of transportation investments. This section explores the importance of diversifying investments across different modes of transport, regions, project types, and risks.

1. Mode Diversification:

Rationale: Investing in a mix of transportation modes, including roads, rail, air, maritime, and emerging technologies.

Benefits:

Risk Mitigation: Reduces dependence on a single mode, minimizing the impact of challenges specific to a particular transportation sector.

Adaptability: Enables adaptation to changing consumer preferences and technological advancements in different transportation modes.

2. Geographical Diversification:

Rationale: Spreading investments across different regions and markets to avoid concentration risks.

Benefits:

Resilience to Economic Shifts: Guards against economic downturns or regulatory changes specific to a particular region.

Market Opportunities: Capitalizes on diverse market conditions, expanding the scope for profitable investments.

3. Project Type Diversification:

Rationale: Balancing investments between large-scale infrastructure projects and smaller, more agile initiatives.

Benefits:

Flexibility: Provides flexibility to adapt to varying project scales, aligning investments with market demands and regulatory changes.

Risk Distribution: Reduces the impact of unforeseen challenges by having a mix of project types with different risk profiles.

4. Risk Diversification:

Rationale: Identifying and diversifying risks associated with economic, regulatory, technological, and environmental factors.

Benefits:

Risk Mitigation: Spreads risks across various categories, minimizing the impact of unexpected events on the overall investment portfolio.

Enhanced Resilience: Builds resilience by avoiding overexposure to specific risk types, ensuring long-term viability.

Implementation Strategies:

Comprehensive Risk Analysis: Conduct thorough risk assessments for each investment, considering economic, regulatory, and environmental factors.

Regular Portfolio Reviews: Periodically review the investment portfolio to assess its alignment with diversification goals and make adjustments as needed.

Strategic Partnerships: Collaborate with partners who bring expertise in different modes, regions, or project types to enhance diversification.

Conclusion:

Diversification is a strategic imperative for long-term success in transportation investments. By carefully balancing investments across various modes, regions, project types, and risks, stakeholders can build a robust portfolio that is adaptable to changing market conditions and resilient in the face of uncertainties.

B. Adapting to Technological Changes:

Overview:

Adapting to technological changes is a critical strategy for ensuring the long-term success of transportation investments. This section explores the importance of continuous technological assessment, collaboration with tech innovators, flexibility in project planning, and data-driven decision-making.

1. Continuous Technological Assessment:

Approach: Establishing mechanisms for ongoing assessment of emerging technologies relevant to the transportation sector.

Benefits:

Strategic Alignment: Ensures that investments remain aligned with the latest technological advancements, optimizing efficiency, safety, and sustainability.

Competitive Edge: Positions stakeholders as early adopters, providing a competitive edge in a rapidly evolving technological landscape.

2. Collaboration with Tech Innovators:

Approach: Actively engaging with technology innovators, startups, and research institutions to stay at the forefront of technological breakthroughs.

Benefits:

Innovation Injection: Injects innovation into projects by tapping into the expertise of tech innovators and staying abreast of cutting-edge developments.

Partnership Opportunities: Creates opportunities for strategic partnerships that can enhance the implementation of transformative technologies.

3. Flexibility in Project Planning:

Approach: Building flexibility into project planning and design to accommodate future technological advancements.

Benefits:

Adaptability: Allows seamless integration of new technologies without significant retrofitting or redevelopment, minimizing disruptions and enhancing project longevity.

Future-Proofing: Enhances the long-term viability of investments by anticipating and accommodating technological changes.

4. Data-Driven Decision-Making:

Approach: Embracing data analytics and leveraging real-time data for informed decision-making.

Benefits:

Operational Efficiency: Improves operational efficiency by utilizing real-time data for traffic management, predictive maintenance, and optimization of transportation systems.

Strategic Insights: Provides valuable insights for optimizing routes, enhancing safety measures, and making informed decisions that contribute to the success of transportation projects.

Implementation Strategies:

Establish Innovation Labs: Create dedicated spaces or partnerships with innovation labs to explore and test emerging technologies.

Regular Training Programs: Keep the workforce updated on technological advancements through regular training programs.

Open Communication Channels: Foster open communication channels with technology providers, allowing for the exchange of ideas and insights.

Conclusion:

Adapting to technological changes is not just a strategy but a necessity in the fast-paced world of transportation. By proactively assessing and embracing emerging technologies, collaborating with innovators, building flexibility into projects, and making data-driven decisions, stakeholders can ensure that their investments remain at the forefront of technological advancements, leading to sustained success in the long term.

C. Sustainable and Responsible Investment Practices:

Overview:

Sustainable and responsible investment practices are foundational for long-term success in the transportation sector. This section explores the importance of environmental impact assessment, social responsibility, ethical governance, and long-term viability assessment.

1. Environmental Impact Assessment:

Practice: Conducting thorough environmental impact assessments for all transportation projects.

Benefits:

Compliance: Demonstrates commitment to regulatory compliance and adherence to environmental standards.

Mitigation of Environmental Risks: Identifies potential environmental risks and allows for the implementation of measures to mitigate negative impacts.

2. Social Responsibility:

Practice: Integrating social responsibility considerations into project planning and execution.

Benefits:

Community Engagement: Fosters positive relationships with communities affected by transportation projects, enhancing public support.

Positive Social Impact: Contributes to social well-being by considering the needs and concerns of local communities.

3. Ethical Governance and Compliance:

Practice: Upholding ethical governance standards and ensuring compliance with all relevant regulations.

Benefits:

Risk Mitigation: Mitigates legal and reputational risks associated with ethical lapses or non-compliance.

Stakeholder Confidence: Builds confidence among investors, stakeholders, and the public by demonstrating a commitment to ethical practices.

4. Long-Term Viability Assessment:

Practice: Incorporating a comprehensive assessment of long-term viability and sustainability in investment decision-making.

Benefits:

Proactive Risk Management: Identifies potential risks and challenges that may arise over the project's lifecycle, allowing for proactive mitigation strategies.

Enhanced Resilience: Ensures that investments are resilient to changing market conditions, technological disruptions, and evolving regulatory landscapes.

Implementation Strategies:

Engage Stakeholders: Actively engage with local communities, NGOs, and regulatory bodies to gather diverse perspectives and ensure responsible decision-making.

Implement Sustainability Standards: Adhere to recognized sustainability standards and certifications to demonstrate a commitment to responsible practices.

Integrate ESG Criteria: Consider Environmental, Social, and Governance (ESG) criteria in investment decisions to align projects with sustainable and responsible principles.

Conclusion:

Sustainable and responsible investment practices are not just ethical considerations; they are integral to the long-term success of transportation investments. By conducting thorough environmental impact assessments, practicing social responsibility, upholding ethical governance, and assessing long-term viability, stakeholders can build projects that not only withstand the test of time but contribute positively to the communities and environments they serve.

Chapter IX: Conclusion

A. Recap of Key Concepts:

As we conclude this exploration into the intricate world of transportation investments, let's recap some of the key concepts that have been discussed throughout this comprehensive guide:

Transportation Landscape:

Understanding the global transportation industry, its key players, and emerging trends that shape the dynamic environment.

Diversification of Investments:

The importance of diversifying investments across various modes of transport, regions, project types, and risks for resilience and adaptability.

Adapting to Technological Changes:

Embracing continuous technological assessment, collaboration with tech innovators, flexibility in project planning, and data-driven decision-making to stay at the forefront of advancements.

Sustainable and Responsible Investment Practices:

Conducting thorough environmental impact assessments, practicing social responsibility, upholding ethical governance, and assessing long-term viability for sustainable and responsible investments.

B. Encouragement for Informed and Strategic Transport Investments:

As we approach the culmination of this exploration into transportation investments, it is essential to extend encouragement to all stakeholders to embrace an informed and strategic approach in their endeavors. The success of transportation investments hinges on a combination of knowledge, foresight, and strategic decision-making. Here is a guide to foster such an approach:

Continuous Learning:

Embrace Knowledge: The world of transportation is dynamic and continually evolving. Commit to continuous learning to stay abreast of emerging technologies, market trends, and regulatory changes.

Invest in Education: Encourage teams to invest in educational programs, training, and industry conferences to foster a culture of continuous learning.

Collaboration:

Forge Partnerships: Foster collaboration among industry players, technology innovators, and regulatory bodies. Collective efforts result in innovation, shared insights, and the development of sustainable solutions.

Knowledge Exchange: Create forums and platforms for knowledge exchange, encouraging stakeholders to share experiences, challenges, and solutions.

Risk-Aware Decision Making:

Diligent Risk Assessment: Recognize that informed decisions involve a thorough understanding and management of risks. Conduct diligent risk assessments and develop robust mitigation strategies.

Adaptive Strategies: Embrace adaptive strategies that allow for the effective management of unforeseen challenges, ensuring resilience in the face of uncertainties.

Technology Integration:

Stay Technologically Current: Acknowledge the transformative impact of technology on transportation. Stay technologically current by actively assessing emerging technologies and integrating them strategically into projects.

Collaborate with Innovators: Actively engage with technology innovators, startups, and research institutions. Collaboration provides access to cutting-edge solutions and enhances technological adoption.

Sustainability as a Guiding Principle:

Beyond Compliance: Recognize sustainability not merely as a regulatory requirement but as a guiding principle. Embrace practices that contribute positively to the environment, society, and the long-term viability of projects.

Social Responsibility: Integrate social responsibility into the fabric of decision-making, ensuring that investments align with community needs and contribute to societal well-being.

Adaptability and Flexibility:

Anticipate Change: Embrace a mindset of adaptability and anticipate change in the transportation landscape. Develop projects with built-in flexibility to accommodate technological advancements and evolving market conditions.

Agile Planning: Adopt agile planning methodologies to facilitate quick responses to changing circumstances, enabling timely adjustments to project trajectories.

In the dynamic field of transportation investments, informed and strategic decision-making is the compass that guides stakeholders through uncharted territories. By promoting continuous learning, collaboration, risk-aware decision-making, technology integration, sustainability, and adaptability, stakeholders can navigate the complexities of the transportation landscape with confidence and contribute to a future characterized by innovation, sustainability, and lasting impact.

C. Final Thoughts on the Future of Transportation Investment:
As we embark on the concluding reflections of this exploration into the future of transportation investment, it is paramount to recognize the transformative potential and pivotal role that strategic investments will play in shaping the future of mobility. Here are some contemplations to encapsulate the essence of the journey:

Technological Renaissance:

A Catalyst for Change: The ongoing technological renaissance in transportation is not merely a phase; it is a catalyst for profound change. From autonomous vehicles to data-driven infrastructure, technology will continue to redefine how we move and connect.

Sustainability as a Guiding Star:
Beyond Compliance: Sustainability is not just a regulatory checkbox; it's a guiding star that should illuminate every decision. Investments that prioritize environmental responsibility and societal well-being will be the cornerstone of a resilient and responsible future.

Human-Centric Approach:
Empowering Communities: The future of transportation investments must be grounded in a human-centric approach. Solutions that enhance accessibility, safety, and the overall quality of life for communities will not only be successful but also contribute meaningfully to societal progress.

Global Collaboration:
Breaking Boundaries: The challenges and opportunities in transportation are not confined by borders. Global collaboration, where stakeholders from different regions and sectors come together, will drive innovation, efficiency, and the creation of interconnected transportation networks.

Adaptive Strategies:

Embracing Change: The future demands adaptive strategies. Embrace change as a constant, and design projects with the flexibility to accommodate unforeseen technological advancements, regulatory shifts, and evolving market dynamics.

Inclusive and Equitable Solutions:

Connecting Everyone: Transportation investments should aim for inclusivity and equity. Projects that connect remote communities, address urban mobility challenges, and bridge socioeconomic gaps will define a future where transportation serves everyone.

Resilience in the Face of Uncertainty:

Building Resilient Systems: Uncertainty is inherent, but resilience is a choice. Future-proof investments by building resilient systems that can withstand economic fluctuations, technological disruptions, and unforeseen challenges.

Legacy of Innovation:

Shaping Tomorrow: Transportation investments have the power to leave a legacy of innovation. Embrace a mindset that goes beyond immediate returns, focusing on projects that not only meet current needs but also contribute to a sustainable and technologically advanced future.

In conclusion, the future of transportation investment is a canvas waiting to be painted with strategic decisions, technological marvels, and a commitment to the well-being of communities and the planet. Stakeholders, armed with knowledge, foresight, and a dedication to innovation, have the opportunity to be architects of a transportation landscape that is not only efficient and economically viable but also environmentally conscious and socially impactful. The journey continues, and the possibilities are limitless.

In conclusion, "Navigating Wealth: A Comprehensive Guide to Strategic Investments in Transportation" serves as a compass for those venturing into the dynamic and evolving realm of transportation investments. This guide has explored the significance of understanding the global transportation industry, embracing diversification, adapting to technological changes, and incorporating sustainable and responsible practices.

Key takeaways from our exploration include:

Holistic Perspective: Successful transportation investments require a holistic understanding of the industry, considering its multifaceted components, stakeholders, and global trends.

Diversification: The strategy of diversifying investments across modes, geographies, and project types is essential for building a resilient and adaptable portfolio.

Technological Adaptation: Embracing technological advancements and fostering a culture of innovation are crucial for staying competitive and future-proofing transportation investments.

Sustainability and Responsibility: Incorporating sustainable and responsible practices not only aligns with global goals but also enhances the long-term viability and positive impact of investments.

Collaboration and Continuous Learning: Collaborative efforts, knowledge exchange, and a commitment to continuous learning are foundational elements for success in the ever-evolving landscape of transportation.

As the transportation industry continues to evolve, stakeholders are encouraged to approach investments with foresight, agility, and a commitment to creating a future where transportation is not just a means of movement but a catalyst for positive change. The journey ahead promises innovation, challenges, and opportunities, and with strategic insights, stakeholders can navigate this landscape with confidence and contribute to a sustainable and prosperous future.